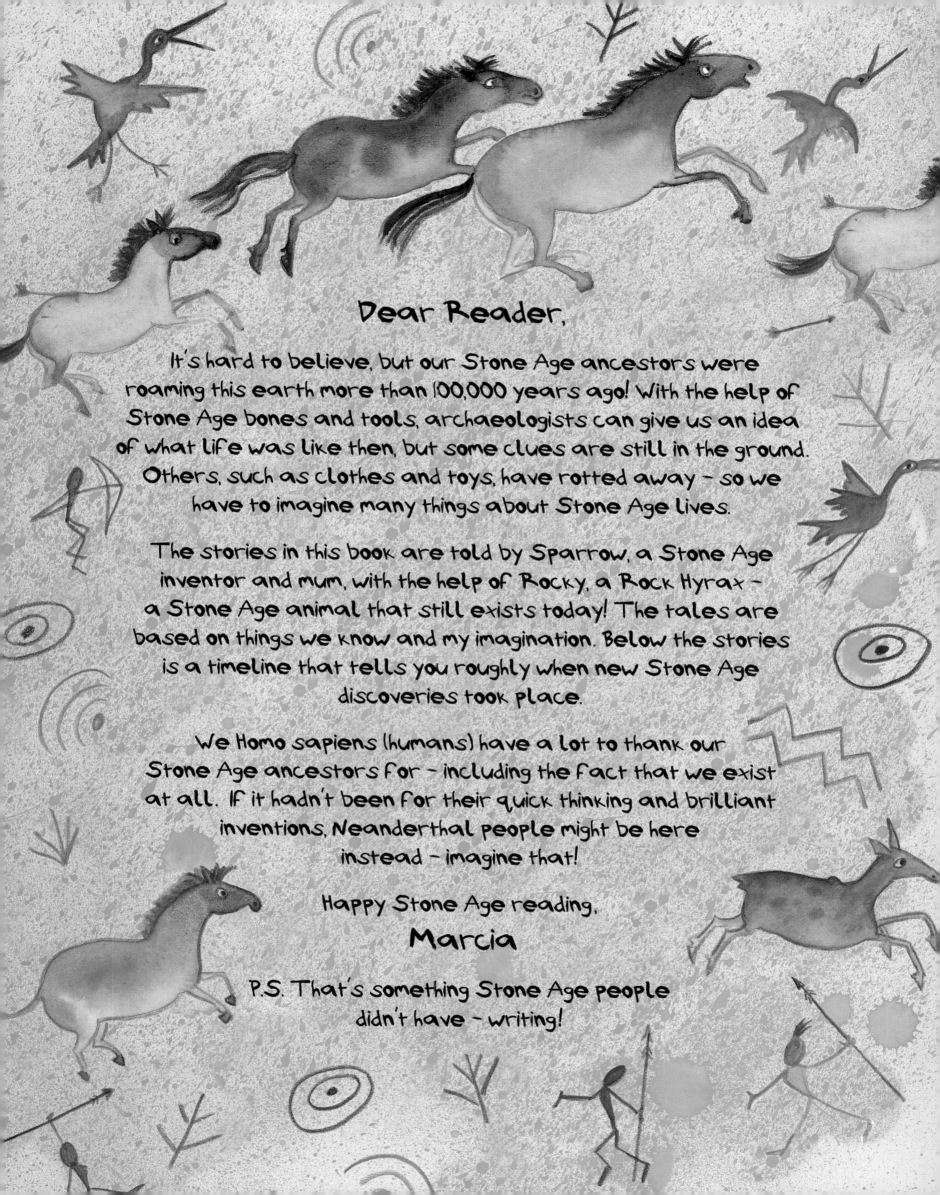

Dear Reader,

It's hard to believe, but our Stone Age ancestors were roaming this earth more than 100,000 years ago! With the help of Stone Age bones and tools, archaeologists can give us an idea of what life was like then, but some clues are still in the ground. Others, such as clothes and toys, have rotted away – so we have to imagine many things about Stone Age lives.

The stories in this book are told by Sparrow, a Stone Age inventor and mum, with the help of Rocky, a Rock Hyrax – a Stone Age animal that still exists today! The tales are based on things we know and my imagination. Below the stories is a timeline that tells you roughly when new Stone Age discoveries took place.

We Homo sapiens (humans) have a lot to thank our Stone Age ancestors for – including the fact that we exist at all. If it hadn't been for their quick thinking and brilliant inventions, Neanderthal people might be here instead – imagine that!

Happy Stone Age reading,
Marcia

P.S. That's something Stone Age people didn't have – writing!

For
May and William
with ugs

First published 2016 by Walker Books Ltd
87 Vauxhall Walk, London SE11 5HJ
2 4 6 8 10 9 7 5 3 1

Text and illustrations © 2016 Marcia Williams

The right of Marcia Williams to be identified as author/illustrator of this work has been
asserted by her in accordance with the Copyright, Designs and Patents Act 1988

This book has been typeset in Truesdell, Rubbish, Kidprint MT, vtks animal 2 and Polymer
Printed in China

British Library Cataloguing in Publication Data:
a catalogue record for this book is available from the British Library

ISBN 978-1-4063-7083-6

www.walker.co.uk

THE STONE AGE

HUNTERS, GATHERERS and WOOLLY MAMMOTHS

Written and illustrated by
MARCIA WILLIAMS

WALKER BOOKS
AND SUBSIDIARIES
LONDON · BOSTON · SYDNEY · AUCKLAND

THE LAST NEANDERTHAL

Did you know that we weren't the first people to walk the earth? The earliest people evolved from apes and started walking upright. Then another people, Homo erectus, discovered how to make stone tools, and the Stone Age began – luckily for us! Otherwise, without spears and knives, we would probably have starved to death or been wiped out by other animals with bigger teeth and stronger muscles. Homo erectus evolved into Homo sapiens – modern humans! We became king of the beasts … but once, long ago, we shared the planet with another kind of people: Neanderthals.

The Neanderthals were descended from apes too, and like us, they lived in small groups, or clans. Their bodies were slow and stocky, they lived mostly in caves, and they were as strong as cave bears! They spoke a strange language that we Homo sapiens didn't understand.

Our clan, Clan Woolly, lived in harmony with the Neanderthals. There was food enough for everyone back then.

OLD STONE AGE

NEANDERTHALS HAD BIG BRAINS, BUT THEY PROBABLY USED MORE BRAINPOWER THAN HOMO SAPIENS TO CONTROL THEIR LARGER BODIES, SO THEY HAD LESS BRAINPOWER FOR LANGUAGE.

PALEOLITHIC PERIOD 120,000–10,000 BC | 120,000 BC | NEANDERTHAL PEOPLE ARE LIVING IN EUROPE AND ASIA.

Then the world grew colder. The land froze and both people and animals struggled to survive.

Wild beasts prowled about trying to steal the clan's food – or even eat clan members!

With each passing moon, food grew scarcer for everyone.

Clan Woolly saw fewer and fewer Neanderthals …

… and more and more bones of starved Neanderthals.

One icy day, the Woollies trapped and speared a sabre-toothed tiger. It was very skinny, but they didn't mind – the meat would still provide a welcome meal after days of hunger and unsuccessful hunting.

HOMO SAPIENS HAD BETTER LANGUAGE SKILLS THAN NEANDERTHALS. EACH CLAN WOULD PROBABLY HAVE DEVELOPED THEIR OWN LANGUAGE.

100,000 BC

HOMO SAPIENS ARE LIVING IN EASTERN AND SOUTHERN AFRICA.

But before the Woollies had even removed their spears from the tiger's body, the cave dwellers attacked. The Woollies fought back with fierce determination — they couldn't afford to lose food to the Neanderthals!

The Neanderthals were weak with hunger and soon lay dead at the Woollies' feet.

Only a wounded Neanderthal mother with a baby in her arms managed to escape.

Those tigers eat anything with legs.

The Woollies piled rocks and snow over the dead. Then they feasted hungrily on the tiger.

They were so busy eating that no one noticed a young girl, Mouse, creep away from the clan.

Yikes! Don't leave the clan, Mouse!

Mouse bravely followed the trail of the Neanderthal mother's blood to the mouth of a cave.

Her little heart pounded, for dusk was falling and she could hear wolves howling close by.

Mouse crept into the furthest and darkest depths of the cave, terrified of what she might find.

Killer bears live in the caves.

THE HOMO SAPIENS WHO LIVED IN CRO-MAGNON LOOKED DIFFERENT FROM HUMANS TODAY. THEIR BODIES WERE HEAVY AND POWERFUL AND THEIR BRAINS WERE BIGGER THAN OURS.

47,000 BC   THE FIRST HOMO SAPIENS IN EUROPE ARE LIVING AT CRO-MAGNON IN FRANCE ALONGSIDE NEANDERTHALS.

This is tense - I'm on the *edge* of my rock!

Mouse found the mother, curled on the ground – dead.

Mouse bent down, took the baby from the mother's arms and ran.

When she came out of the cave she heard the wolves close behind her.

Wolves eat hyraxes.

The baby wailed, the wolves howled and Mouse screamed. She prayed her father would hear.

As the wolves attacked Mouse, a spear suddenly whistled through the air towards them.

Wolves eat people!

No, he's mine!

Mouse's father had come! He pulled her into the safety of his arms. Then he grabbed hold of the Neanderthal baby and tried to throw him to the wolves – but Mouse would not give up her prize.

There are lots of us. Yippee!

Tey enog ton ev'ew.

Well, it won't be long now.

Yllaudarg tuo eid ot desoppus er'ew!

WE DON'T KNOW WHEN MAN FIRST MADE CLOTHES, BUT NEANDERTHALS AND HOMO SAPIENS COULDN'T HAVE SURVIVED THE ICE AGE WITHOUT THEM!

42,000 BC

HOMO SAPIENS MULTIPLY. NEANDERTHALS GRADUALLY DIE OUT.

None of the Woollies wanted the strange, wailing baby in the clan.

Then he yawned and gurgled, just like any other baby.

Mouse's mother held him. He grabbed her finger and smiled.

Hyrax motto: never bring a strange baby home.

Still, it all ended happily ever after...

Except for the Neanderthals. They became extinct!

Mouse named the baby Root. He grew to be a strong, fearless hunter. The Woollies never saw another Neanderthal and they believed that Root was the last of his kind. Mind you, when Root grew up he married a woman from Clan Woolly and many of their children, so I am told, were stocky and as strong as cave bears!

PEOPLE STARTED MAKING SMALL SCULPTURES CALLED VENUS FIGURINES, MAYBE FOR SPIRITUAL REASONS OR MAYBE BECAUSE HUMANS ARE CREATIVE!

MAMMOTH HUNTERS ARE FOUND IN THE CZECH REPUBLIC. MORE HOMO SAPIENS SETTLE IN AUSTRALIA.

HUNTER-GATHERERS

Another story, please.

Hunter-gatherers lived a tough life. They were nomads (they moved around rather than living in one place) and they spent their days searching for plants to eat and hunting wild creatures. Houses didn't exist yet — they sheltered in caves or built huts from branches and animal skins. No one knew how to make fire, so clans had to wait for lightning to strike before they could cook. Good hunters were important in a clan, and so were people who could make tools and weapons out of stone. Bears, sabre-toothed cats and other beasts lurked everywhere — you were as likely to be eaten as to eat!

If this is supper, I'm leaving.

Can I come?

During the Ice Age, every day was a struggle against cold and hunger. Some Woolly members left the clan and joined other tribes with more food!

Can I stay?

Oh, yes!

So long as you can hunt.

Fern's in love!

But one summer, when even a bitter-tasting ant was a treat, a strong young man named Garth joined Clan Woolly from another tribe.

Sorry, I tripped!

You're no use now.

Oh, he is!

No work, no food – leave!

The Woollies were weak from hunger, so someone to help them hunt and build shelters was welcome — but after a few passing moons, Garth broke his spear arm.

It's a sign, let him stay.

Cooked ant, anyone?

FIRE!!!

The men were about to force him to leave when lightning struck a tree! The Woollies were so excited to have fire that they forgot about Garth and he stayed.

Life's a struggle.

Sometimes we shelter in caves.

Sometimes, we find fire.

Sometimes we make animal-skin shelters.

We're nearly always cold and hungry.

DURING THE ICE AGE, MUCH OF THE LAND AND WATER WAS FROZEN, SO FOOD AND WATER WAS LIMITED. IT IS A MIRACLE PEOPLE SURVIVED AT ALL!

16,000 BC   THE ICE AGE IS AT ITS COLDEST. SOME ANIMALS BEGIN TO STRUGGLE. OTHERS THRIVE.

The Woollies made flaming torches and chased a bison into a pit. Now they had enough meat for days and fire to cook it on, so they could relax at last. The clan found a cave and rested for the first time in weeks.

Have you ever seen a hyrax in a cave painting?

The answer is no!

How insulting is that!

Fern was very glad that Garth stayed with the Woollies — she was having his baby! Fern was the Woollies' cave painter. At night, Garth kept the fire going while she decorated the walls. She made her colours by mixing charcoal from the fire and red ochre from the cliffs with spit and animal fat. Usually, she and Garth would sing together all night long — but one night they both fell asleep and the fire went out!

CAVE PAINTERS APPLIED COLOURS WITH LICHEN, MOSS, TWIGS, FEATHERS AND THEIR FINGERS. SOME USED HORSEHAIR BRUSHES TOO.

15,000 BC

CAVE PAINTINGS AND BONE AND ANTLER CARVINGS ARE MADE IN EUROPE.

I want to be a hibernating bear, not a hunter-gatherer!

With no fire and little food, the Woollies had to set out again after the migrating reindeer.

My arm's nearly healed.

It better be.

Reindeer were difficult to hunt – and the clan were struggling without Garth's spear skills.

Don't eat that wolf lichen, it's poisonous.

For days, the clan lived off lichen and the occasional bird. Fern grew hungrier and her belly grew bigger.

Yes, hunger makes you moody as well as mean.

Hungry bears can't hibernate – and boy, does that make them moody!

This clan is one meal away from starvation!

Our baby's like a tiny bird.

There's a bear up there.

We need fire!

It must be too hungry to hibernate.

When Fern's baby was due, the clan made camp in the shelter of some rocks and she gave birth to a tiny girl named Wings. That night, a cave bear was spotted lurking in the shadows, drawn by the smell of the newborn baby. The bear was hungry and the clan could hear it prowling all through the night.

I've drawn you some extinct animals.

DOEDICURUS

WOOLLY RHINO

REIGOMYS

EREMOTHERIUM

HOMO SAPIENS WERE WASTEFUL HUNTERS. THEY SOMETIMES DROVE A WHOLE HERD OVER A CLIFF JUST TO EAT ONE ANIMAL.

15,000 BC

MANY PLANTS, MAMMALS AND BIRDS BEGIN TO DIE OUT DURING THIS PERIOD.

In the morning, a band of hunters set off after the reindeer – an easier kill than the bear.

Others, including Garth, stayed behind to protect the young in case the bear attacked.

After many hours, the hunters managed to chase two reindeer to the edge of a cliff.

They edged forwards until the two deer went crashing to their deaths on the jagged rocks below. By the time the hunters had climbed down to fetch their kill, one deer had already been dragged away by wolves. But the other deer would feed the whole clan for a week. It was a successful hunt and a happy day!

MANY ANIMALS ADAPTED TO THE WARMER CLIMATE AND ARE STILL AROUND TODAY — INCLUDING HOMO SAPIENS!

THIS IS PROBABLY DUE TO CLIMATE CHANGE: THE WORLD IS GETTING WARMER.

The food cheered everyone up, except Fern. She was scared the bear would return for Wings.

So early the next morning, the hunters decided to track down the bear and try to kill it.

But the bear had been hiding above Fern's shelter and when the hunters left, it pounced!

Only Garth was there to fight it. He threw himself between Fern, Wings and the bear.

Forgetting about his weak arm, he lifted a great rock and smashed it onto the beast's skull.

The bear let out a howl, staggered a few paces and then attacked Garth again.

Garth lifted the rock a second time and hurled it at the bear. He knocked the beast off its feet.

Garth seized the moment. He took his knife and killed the bear. Fern sighed – Wings was safe at last.

MANY OF THE SKELETONS FOUND IN THE GRAVE WERE WOMEN. THEY HAD ARROWHEADS EMBEDDED IN THEM.

15,000 BC   THE FIRST EVIDENCE OF WAR IS FOUND IN A GRAVE BY THE RIVER NILE IN EGYPT.

Garth was badly slashed and bruised and his broken arm hung uselessly by his side — it would never heal. He would never hunt or make tools again. But he had saved Wings from the bear and even the hunters were awed by his bravery. He was finally welcomed as a member of Clan Woolly and everyone celebrated — except Wings, who slept on, unaware that her dad was a hero!

THE FIRST-KNOWN CLAY ITEMS WERE NOT POTS BUT LITTLE CLAY ANIMALS. THEY MIGHT HAVE BEEN TOYS OR IMAGES OF ANIMAL SPIRITS.

Hunter-gatherers don't make many pots.

Pots don't travel well.

You have to fire (bake) them for ages.

Little animals are easy to fire.

They're easy to carry, too!

11,500 BC

PEOPLE MAKE POTS OUT OF CLAY, BUT THEY ARE VERY FRAGILE.

THE MIRACLE OF FIRE!

Hyraxes didn't enjoy the Ice Age!

Listen to my warming tale!

Can you imagine, Shrimp, how miserable it must have been before fire was tamed? It would have been freezing at night, and completely dark when there was no moon. Without fire there was no protection from insects or wild animals — and worst of all, food was always raw! Just think — raw meat, roots and wild vegetation. Some of it was almost impossible to digest. It was lucky for us that people worked out how to make fire before you and I were born. Otherwise my brilliant cooking skills would have been wasted and your poor toes would have dropped off in the cold!

Hunter-gobblers like us prefer a warm climate.

Your great-great-great granny was always cold and never sat down!

Was she bonkers?

The Ice Age eventually ended and the land became warmer. Clan Woolly still moved around, especially in the winter, when there was less food about.

Look, I found some honey.

And some blinkin' bees!

In summer, they camped near water where they fished, hunted, scavenged for dead animals and gathered berries, grain, birds' eggs and roots.

Gobble gobble!

I may be old, but no one can shape an axe, arrowhead, scraper, spearhead or antler hammer as skilfully as me!

SHOW OFF!

In winter, the clan moved to more sheltered areas, carrying any dried meat, fish and grain they'd saved over the summer. They had more time for making tools and weapons during the colder months. Their skilled tool maker, our ancestor, Old Snore, was vital to the clan — and he knew it!

MIDDLE STONE AGE

Sun!

Fire!

Nice!

Aaaaagh, the ground is melting.

Where's my ice?

AS THE ICE RETREATED, PEOPLE COULD MOVE AROUND MORE EASILY. HOMO SAPIENS BEGAN TO TRAVEL ALL ACROSS THE WORLD.

MESOLITHIC PERIOD 10,000–5,000 BC

10,000 BC

THE LAST GLACIAL PERIOD ENDS AND THE CLIMATE BECOMES WARMER.

Unfortunately, Old Snore refused to pass on his skills — even to his grandson, Stump.

Stump was eager to learn and was always bashing stones and asking questions.

His poor hands and legs were permanently covered with bruises and flint cuts!

One night, Stump slipped a hand into the bag of tools under Old Snore's head and tried to take some flint.

Old Snore woke up and whacked Stump so hard that he bounced off the ground!

Stump had had enough. He grabbed his wooden spear and ran from the camp — a bad plan, as hungry beasts were on the prowl.

By dawn, there was still no sign of Stump. His father went to search for him, but he returned with nothing but a rabbit.

ANIMALS LIKE THE WOOLLY MAMMOTH STRUGGLE TO ADAPT TO THE WARMER CLIMATE.

That night, Old Snore took his spear and crept from the camp.

He guessed that Stump had gone to look for flint on Rockslide Hill.

He struggled up the hill until he saw a trail of smoke.

You were *definitely* too hard on the boy.

As Old Snore scrambled over a rise he saw Stump fast asleep – beside a blazing fire.

Stump told him he'd made the fire himself and could do it again. Old Snore shook his head in disbelief.

Fire's too precious to man to joke about.

Stump couldn't convince Old Snore that he was telling the truth. He angrily scuffed out the fire, picked up his things and ran away.

Stump didn't stop running until he reached Clan Woolly's camp. Then he grabbed the gathering shell and blew it loudly.

Fire is scary. It can chase you through grass.

PEOPLE COOKED MEAT ON SPITS OVER FIRES. THEY ALSO BAKED FOOD ON FLAT ROCKS PLACED ON A FIRE. COOKED FOOD WAS EASIER TO DIGEST.

10,000 BC   AS THE USE OF BOWS AND ARROWS SPREADS, HUNTING BECOMES EASIER AND SAFER.

When Old Snore puffed into camp, his grandson made him sit down next to him. Stump took a flat piece of wood and a tuft of dried moss, and he fitted his wooden spear into a groove in the wood. He took Old Snore's hands in his, and twisted the spear faster and faster until smoke started rising and the moss caught fire. Slowly, Stump added twigs and dried grass until there was a proper blaze. The Woollies all cheered and Old Snore almost smiled. He mumbled and grumbled, but finally he promised to show Stump how to make a flint spear tip … just so that he could keep his old wooden spear as a fire stick!

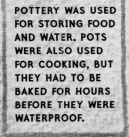

9,000 BC

MORE PEOPLE LEARN TO MAKE FIRE. POTTERY BECOMES STRONGER AND MORE DURABLE.

MAN'S BEST FRIEND

The trouble with people is they think too much.

Wake up, this is my favourite tale.

The very first animals that Homo sapiens tamed were wolves. Wolves may not look like us, but their lives are quite similar. They live in extended family groups; they obey a dominant wolf (just like we obey our clan chief); and they would do anything to protect their pups! Later in the Stone Age, all sorts of other wild animals, such as sheep, goats and pigs, were domesticated, but that was so we wouldn't have to hunt them — wolves were different. They evolved into dogs and became man's best friend. And the first person to tame them was a girl named Leaf — or so the story goes…

Hyraxes don't do sorrow or graves.

She's still awake.

Are you listening, Leaf?

The tale of Stump discovering fire became a clan favourite.

Say something, Leafy!

Leaf would listen to the story, as still as a wild creature.

It's sad, Leaf, but we have to talk!

Her mother had died, and she had hardly spoken since.

Hyraxes eat, sleep and die - simple!

She's dead, silly. Why would she want flowers?

Leaf spent hours scattering flowers on her mother's grave.

Although Leaf didn't speak, she whistled to animals and birds.

Silly. Birds are for eating!

Once she tried to heal an injured bird, but her father broke its neck.

I started by catching a couple of lambs and rearing them.

Now he's got a friendly flock!

And who shepherds the flock?

SHEEP AND GOATS WERE REALLY IMPORTANT AS THEY PROVIDED CLOTHES, MILK, CHEESE AND MEAT. HERDING ANIMALS MEANT THESE THINGS WERE ALWAYS AVAILABLE.

8,500 BC

PEOPLE BEGIN TO HERD SHEEP AND GOATS IN MESOPOTAMIA (MODERN IRAQ).

One evening, as the clan sat by the fire, a pack of wolves tried to steal the kill the hunters had brought home that day. The wolves were hungry and wouldn't leave – until Leaf's father had speared one of them.

The wolf was a female, heavy with milk. Leaf's father skinned her and gave the warm pelt to Leaf.

Leaf curled into a ball on top of the pelt, her eyes full of tears.

The next morning, Leaf and the pelt were gone. The clan searched for days, but as the summer leaves turned brown, even Leaf's father stopped looking for her. The Woollies started the journey to their winter camp without her – the reindeer were migrating and the clan had to follow.

JERICHO WAS BUILT IN A DESERT NEAR AN OASIS. THE HOUSES WERE MADE OUT OF MUD BRICKS AND THERE WAS A STONE WALL AROUND THE TOWN TO STOP WILD ANIMALS GETTING IN.

8,000 BC

A TOWN IS BUILT AT JERICHO IN THE MIDDLE EAST.

The snow came early that year and hunting was difficult. The Woollies grew hungry.

Days went by without a kill. Cold and hunger gnawed deep at every clan member.

One morning the clan were woken by whistling — it was Leaf with three young wolves!

She kept her distance and warned the clan not to harm her wolves. The wolves stayed close to Leaf.

Leaf beckoned the clan to follow her, but they were nervous and kept a spear's length from the wolves.

She led the Woollies to the carcass of a reindeer that the wolves had killed. The Woollies expected the wolves to guard the dead reindeer, but instead they lay at Leaf's feet and didn't try to stop the clan carrying the reindeer to the camp.

A DUGOUT CANOE IS MADE FROM ONE LOG OF WOOD. IT'S THE OLDEST KNOWN KIND OF BOAT, BUT EARLIER ONES MAY HAVE BEEN MADE FROM BARK OR ANIMAL SKIN.

6,500 BC

PEOPLE IN THE NETHERLANDS MAKE DUGOUT CANOES.

The night she left, Leaf had taken the wolf mother's pelt and gone to find the cubs. Smelling their mother, the cubs had followed Leaf and she had fed and trained them. She hadn't returned to the clan because she feared the Woollies would kill the cubs.

The clan were nervous of having Leaf's wolves living amongst them, but they very soon realized the benefits. The wolves were amazing hunters and helped to feed the clan, and they were loyal and barked when danger approached. Sometimes they even kept a chosen clan member warm at night! Leaf had named her wolves Star, Sky and Flower, and when Sky gave birth to a litter, the other Woollies queued for the pups. Little whistling Leaf had found man's best friend — and they had helped her find her voice!

BRITAIN WAS TURNED INTO AN ISLAND BY RISING SEA LEVELS. A LANDSLIDE IN NORWAY PROBABLY TRIGGERED A HUGE TSUNAMI WHICH STRUCK BRITAIN AND FLOODED LOW-LYING LAND.

6,100 BC

BRITAIN IS CUT OFF FROM EUROPE AND BECOMES AN ISLAND.

FROM NOMADS TO FARMERS

Hyraxes do not like change.

Farmers didn't suddenly appear with all the knowledge they needed to grow food and tame animals. Like most big changes, farming grew from many small beginnings. First, the earth's climate changed, so that it was warm enough for crops to grow. Over time, toolmaking improved, making it possible to clear and prepare land for farming. Most importantly, people learned more about the seasons and how plants grow. Nomadic people who moved from place to place slowly realized that they could shape the wildness of nature and live a more settled life.

Grub and his wife, Starling, belonged to Clan Woolly, but they were loners and had disgusting manners. Their children, Fox and Toad, did too!

The Grubs knew where to find water, how to read animal tracks and what plants were safe to eat, but they knew little about clan behaviour.

Then one year, when the clan was preparing for the winter migration, Grub's family refused to mix their wild grain into the carrying bags.

Everyone thought they were joking, but they surrounded their grain and raised their spears, threatening anyone who came close.

It was enough to shrink from bison size to mouse size!

Give us a rock and we're happy.

LATE STONE AGE

SEA LEVELS KEPT RISING AND AREAS OF SOUTH-EAST ASIA WERE CUT OFF FROM THE MAINLAND. NEW GUINEA AND TASMANIA WERE SEPARATED FROM AUSTRALIA.

NEOLITHIC PERIOD 5,000–2,000 BC

5,000 BC

RICE FARMING STARTS IN EASTERN CHINA AND SPREADS TO INDIA.

The most important clan law is the sharing of food, so as Grub and his family would not be persuaded to share theirs, the clan left for the winter migration without them.

They thought the Grubs would follow, as a lone family couldn't survive a winter.

The clan kept a lookout, but the days went by without any sign of the Grubs.

As usual, the winter was long and hard, but eventually the first signs of spring arrived.

All the Woollies were excited about returning to their summer camp — but on the way, they came across a scattering of human bones.

The clan was convinced that the bones belonged to the Grubs — so when they reached the hill above the camp, they were startled to see smoke rising.

INTEREST IN FARMING CONTINUED TO GROW. BY THIS TIME, WHEAT FARMING HAD SPREAD TO NORTH-WEST EUROPE AND RICE FARMING HAD SPREAD TO INDIA.

4,400 BC

WILD HORSES ARE DOMESTICATED IN RUSSIA.

The clan crept cautiously down the hill and peered through the bushes, astonished by what they saw. Part of the land had been cleared of trees, and smoke came drifting from a wooden shelter unlike anything they had seen before. The Woollies approached with caution, thinking a new tribe had taken the area, but it was the Grub family – not bones, but very much alive! The Grubs had never set off for the winter camp and had managed to survive on their own in the summer camp. They even had a new young one!

A megalith is a huge stone used to build a monument.

This is how we use logs to move them.

This is how we use them to build a tomb.

4,200 BC

MEGALITHIC TOMBS ARE BUILT IN WESTERN EUROPE.

The Grubs had planted their grain on the cleared land and green shoots were just pushing through. They had built fences to keep wild animals from attacking them or damaging their crops. Some Woollies thought the Grubs were mad. Others decided to join them and try farming too. They built permanent shelters and planted seeds. They stored dried fish, meat and grain to last through the winter. It seemed brave at the time, but now most clans are farmers and only a few follow the reindeer. All thanks to the disgusting Grubs!

THE PLOUGH AND THE WHEEL WERE INVENTED IN THE MIDDLE EAST. THESE INVENTIONS TRANSFORMED FARMING AND QUICKLY SPREAD TO EUROPE.

4,000 BC

WOOL IS USED FOR TEXTILES.

3,500 BC

THE PLOUGH AND WHEEL ARE INVENTED.

THE END OF THE STONE AGE

No more cakes unless you listen to a story about me!

What about *my* story?

So, Shrimp, now you know all about the Stone Age — except how it ended! The Stone Age lasted about 3.4 million years, until bronze was discovered. After that, stone tools went out of fashion. Bronze is stronger than stone and much easier to shape and sharpen, so bronze ploughs, knives and other tools are more efficient. That means a farm can feed more people with fewer workers. Other new inventions like the wheel (for transport) and the potters' wheel (for making pottery) have also made life easier. This is the dawn of another exciting new era: the Bronze Age!

I'm with her on mud baths, though.

I'm Sparrow!

   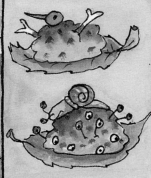

I have told you many tales of my ancestors, but this story is about me, Sparrow, and how I brought an end to the Stone Age. I am not just a storyteller — I am also an inventor! When I was little, I invented mud pots, mud make-up, mud baths and best of all, mud cakes!

At least she doesn't make hyrax cakes!

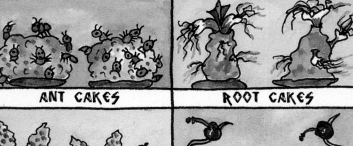

ANT CAKES   ROOT CAKES   WORM CAKES   FISH CAKES

LICE CAKES   MICE CAKES   SMILEY CAKES   GRUMPY CAKES

The cakes were such a success I decided to specialize in them, using wheat instead of mud. Delicious!

I prefer the desert!

THE FIRST SAILING SHIPS USED ON THE RIVER NILE IN EGYPT HAD SQUARE SAILS. THE BOATS THEMSELVES WERE MADE OF PAPYRUS REEDS. THEY WERE STEERED BY OARS.

3,500 BC   THE FIRST CITIES ARE BUILT IN MESOPOTAMIA.   3,400 BC   SHIPS ARE SAILED ON THE NILE.

I was, without doubt, the best cook in our clan and I was always trying out new ideas for recipes.

I was born when farming was our way of life, so I had lots of time and plenty of food to experiment with!

When my friend One-eye tied the knot, I invented four totally new recipes for the occasion. We celebrated with sizzled fish eyes on fish scale bread; five fried bugs: ants, beetles, spiders, scorpions and crickets in bone marrow jelly; gut and gore stew; nettle gloop; and we finished with ... wait for it ... baby baboon, berry and bird-bone cake. Everyone came back for seconds – and even thirds!

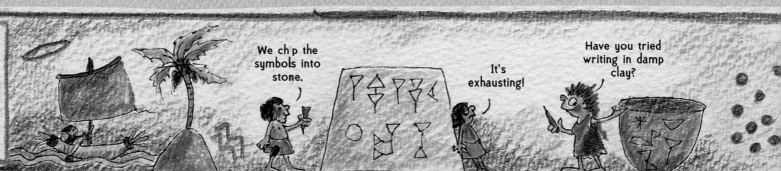

AS WRITING SPREAD, THE PERIOD KNOWN AS PREHISTORY GRADUALLY ENDED. PEOPLE STARTED WRITING ABOUT IMPORTANT EVENTS AND RECORDED HISTORY BEGAN!

3,300 BC

THE FIRST SYSTEM OF WRITING DEVELOPS IN MESOPOTAMIA.

But my greatest recipe was yet to come. Our lives had been steadily changing for years, as more clans began to farm. Small settlements grew into villages and then into towns. Animals that we once hunted were now tame, and we kept sheep, goats, pigs and cattle in fenced areas. We produced more food, so not everyone had to farm – craftspeople, priests, traders, cooks and inventors were born. People shared ideas, and religion became more organized. Shrines were built, as well as stone monuments where people could gather. And then one day I started a whole new era – completely by accident!

3,000 BC

THE CONSTRUCTION OF THE STONEHENGE MONUMENT BEGINS IN ENGLAND.

STONEHENGE WAS BUILT OVER MANY CENTURIES. THE SUN SHINES THROUGH IT AT SUNRISE ON MIDSUMMER AND SUNSET ON MIDWINTER.

I wanted to try out a new bread recipe, and I had scoured the land for stones that would heat the dough to the perfect temperature. I built an oven and set my fire – and then I noticed the veins in some of the stones melting and joining together, forming a hard, flat substance which I named copper. Copper was perfect for removing the bread from the oven, and I discovered many other uses for it too. Soon everyone wanted some copper, so I gave up cooking and started to make copper tools. I mixed the copper with tin which made an even stronger substance: bronze. Now, nobody uses stone tools. Bronze ones are just so much better!

BRONZE WASN'T JUST USED TO MAKE TOOLS AND WEAPONS. IT WAS ALSO USED TO MAKE DECORATIVE ITEMS SUCH AS BROOCHES AND USEFUL THINGS SUCH AS SAFETY PINS!

The bronze axe!

The bronze spear tip!

The bronze arrowhead!

The bronze brooch!

Hello Bronze Age!

Goodbye Stone Age!

2,000 BC

BRONZE, WHICH FIRST APPEARED IN 4,000 BC, IS NOW BEING USED BY MOST PEOPLE.

Marcia Williams

With her distinctive cartoon-strip style, lively text and brilliant wit,
Marcia Williams brings to life colourful historical characters and some of the
world's all-time favourite stories. Her hilarious retellings and clever observations
will have children laughing out loud and coming back for more!

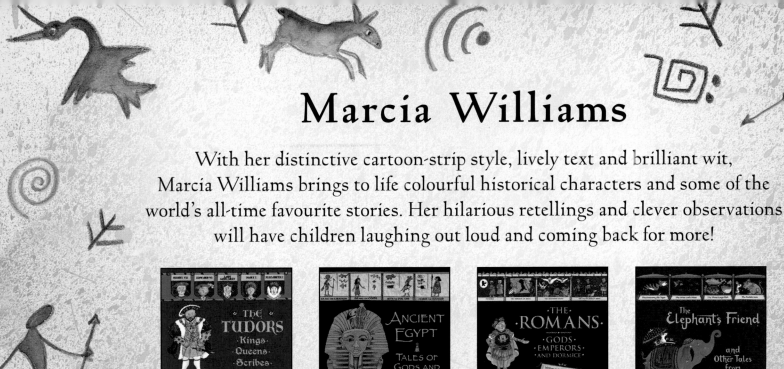

ISBN 978-1-4063-5945-9   ISBN 978-1-4063-3832-4   ISBN 978-1-4063-5455-3   ISBN 978-1-4063-4492-9

ISBN 978-1-4063-2334-4   ISBN 978-1-4063-2335-1   ISBN 978-1-4063-6661-7   ISBN 978-1-4063-6660-0

ISBN 978-1-4063-6102-5   ISBN 978-1-4063-4694-7   ISBN 978-1-4063-5268-9   ISBN 978-1-4063-3199-8

ISBN 978-1-4063-0348-3   ISBN 978-1-4063-0563-0   ISBN 978-1-4063-0562-3   ISBN 978-1-4063-6086-8

Available from all good booksellers

www.walker.co.uk